There is a town in the mountains not
far from here where people lock their
pianos on the night of the full moon.
It makes no difference – the keys
move up and down and the air
is filled with wild music.

Someone once thought
they saw a white bird flying
between the trees. But the truth
of the matter is that it's not a bird
that flies on the night of the full moon
but a pair of white gloves. I know this
because they used to belong to me...

KidGlovz

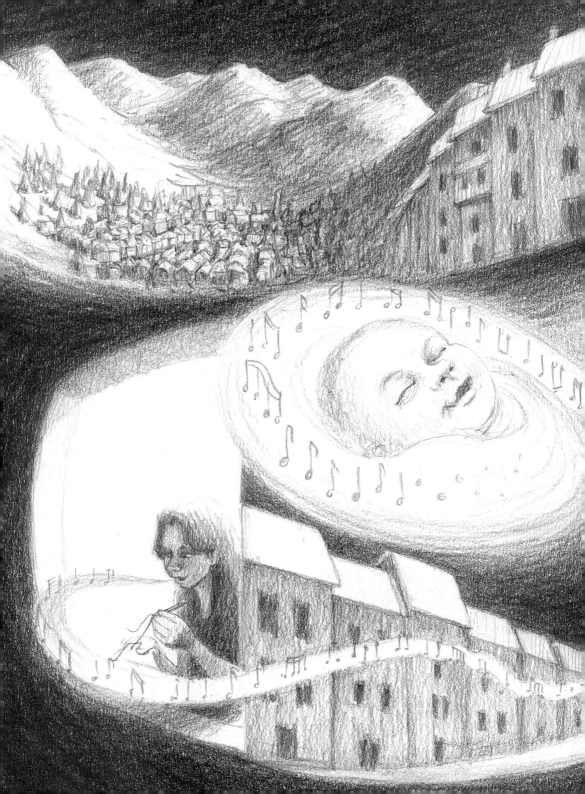

To Raphie and
Jenny Peck
J.H.

For Alison and
Raphael — my angels
D.N.

KidGlovz

STORY BY JULIE HUNT
ILLUSTRATIONS BY DALE NEWMAN

ALLEN&UNWIN
SYDNEY·MELBOURNE·AUCKLAND·LONDON

PART I

Good evening, ladies and gentlemen. It is my very great pleasure to introduce tonight's performer — a boy wonder, a wonderchild . . .
CADENZA STATE THEATRE

The boy is tiny but his talent is huge. Behind me you will see that the piano has been specially altered so his little feet can reach the pedals. At two years of age he played the Minute Waltz in thirteen seconds. At three he began composing the first of his major concertos. And now, at six years of age, he is at the height of his powers.

THE CONCERT WAS A TRIUMPH.

AFTER THE CONCERT

My opening passage was good but I messed up bar 56. I hope Spin didn't notice.

DR ERONIOUS SPIN
IMPRESARIO
(MD, PHD, CCPDE)

MIRACLE CURES
HYPNOTISM
FINANCIAL ADVICE

CADENZA TOWERS

This job is too much for me.

I wish Spin would let me play my own compositions.

Here's dinner. Now three hours' sleep and then you must start practising again.

Grimwade, I'm tired.

I can't help that. I'm just doing my job.

Poor little mite. It's not much of a life.

KIDGLOVZ HEARD MUSIC PLAYING IN HIS MIND EVERY MOMENT OF THE DAY. WHEN HIS FINGERS TOUCHED THE KEYBOARD THE POWER OF MUSIC RAN UP THROUGH HIS HANDS INTO HIS ARMS LIKE ELECTRICITY. IT FILLED HIS BODY AND HIS MIND. BUT SOMETIMES, AFTER A CONCERT, MUSIC WAS NOT ENOUGH.

23

Is this silver?

I suppose so.

Good.
Gee, you're all
dressed up!

I've been
performing.

What's with
the gloves?

Have you always been a tightrope walker?

Among other things. At the moment I'm a thief. I can't steal a piano though, and you don't seem to have anything else.

You could steal me!

I've got to go. It's been good to meet you, KidGlovz.

LOVEGROVE'S HOUSE

34

Come in.
Come in.

Not you.

BANG!

35

37

Now if you will excuse me, dear sister, I have business to attend to.

It had to happen, eventually.

AARRRO OOOO

NO, NO, NO.
That won't do.
Make him look younger.
You'll have to do the
illustration again.

I need you to make
a piano that's oversized so
the pianist looks smaller.

It's an unusual request.
It will take a year.

A YEAR! The boy's
growing like a weed.
His career could be
over in a year. I need
the piano now.

That's not
possible!

Maybe this will help.

It's getting too tight for him. Can you let out the shoulder seams without making the coat look any bigger?

I'll try, sir, but I think he'll need a new one. He's growing.

Strange how the boy never needs new gloves. They seem to grow with him.

Cut down his food, Mr Grimwade. You're giving him far too much.

He's hardly eating enough to keep a sparrow alive.

You heard me.

Yes, boss.

41

43

KidGlovz, get practising!

You've got a competition next month and if you don't win your life won't be worth living.

45

48

Then go further.
Go to the other side
of the world.

I'd have to
take the piano.

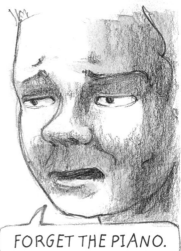

FORGET THE PIANO.

I need to play. It's all
I've ever done. Anyway
I can't leave. Grimwade is
always watching me.

49

Dear Lovegrove,

I'm writing a piece of music and dedicating it to you. It may be my last. I'm not getting enough to eat. I miss you and Hugo very much. The only good thing in my life now is that I have a friend. His name is Shoestring and he will deliver this note. I've never had a friend before. He comes to me along a rope. I guess it is only a matter of time before Spin finds out and cuts it.

Love,

KidGlovz

x x x x

55

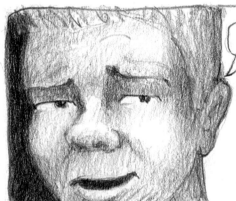

What happened?

I had an injury, an accident...

56

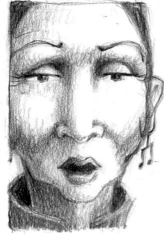

But now I am a teacher, a very good teacher. I am the best in Cadenza.

Thank you for doing this, Shoestring. I hope it is going to work out...

I hope so too.

Trust me. Everything will be fine.

I don't want anyone to get hurt.

Just leave it to me.

PART II

CLACK-ET-TY   CLACK-ET-TY

That ought to stop it. Now we wait.

The train should be here by midnight.

I wish you hadn't brought the boy. You know I don't like working with children.

Once we get the loot he'll change his mind. I'll be part of the gang!

You're coming too, Big Belly.

Spin will kill me if I lose the boy.

LOVEGROVE'S HOUSE

CADENZA TOWERS

I smell a rat, Grimwade. Are you sure you've told me everything?

Yes, boss, everything.

It takes a rat to smell a rat.

Go and get some potatoes to make up the weight. He's a valuable boy but he's not worth a whole sack of coins.

CADENZA STATION

This is it. This is the spot.

Excuse me sir, but this is not a station.

This is where we get off.

Which way, Grimwade?

Up.

This would never have happened if you had done your job properly.

83

It's just a scratch. Nothing serious.

NO DEAL! You keep him. Grimwade, pick up my property.

DROP IT.

You're a fool, Grimwade. You're sacked.

This has been a complete botch-up. I'll never do a kidnapping again.
Come on, you've got to eat.
NO, NO. Every note must be perfect.
Please, Kid. Try and eat. Just one mouthful.
If I eat I will grow... and if I grow he will notice...

CRESCENDO! There are too many notes in the chord!

He's not making sense.

He's raving.

More left hand... B minor!

Mmmmm... a sweet melody.

He needs to keep warm. Have you got a spare blanket?

That's good, KidGlovz. You've nearly finished it. Now rest.

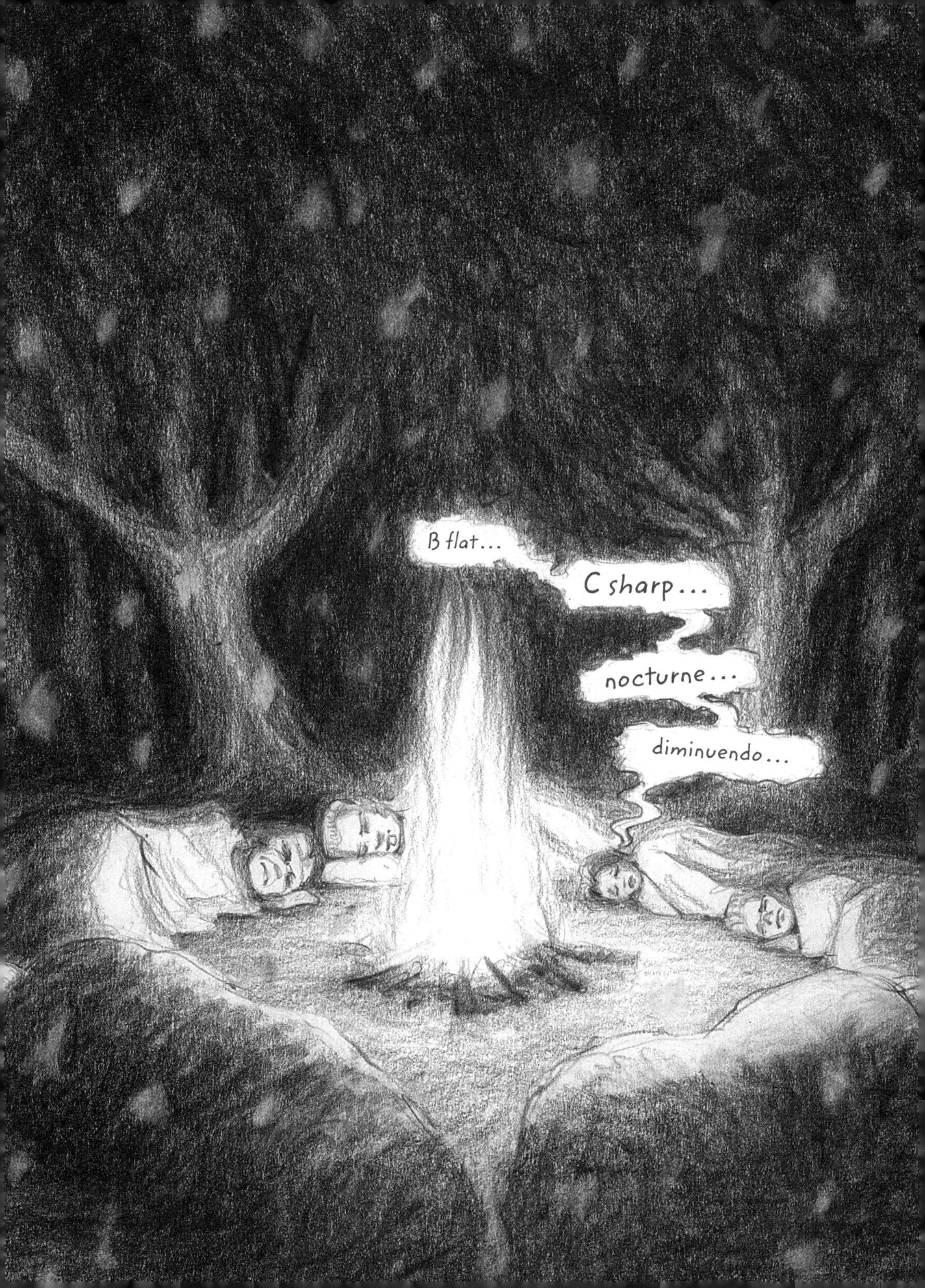

B flat...
C sharp...
nocturne...
diminuendo...

I don't think I can do it, Shoestring. I feel weak.

Give him the music.

It's called Count Arpeggio's Tragical Symphony for Piano and Six Hands.

But he's only got two...

And one of them is hurt.

He's all right. Go ahead.

105

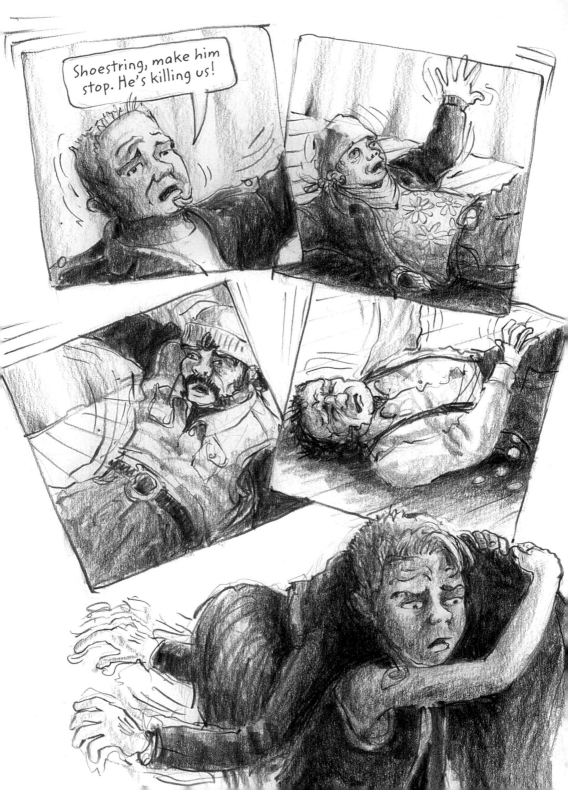

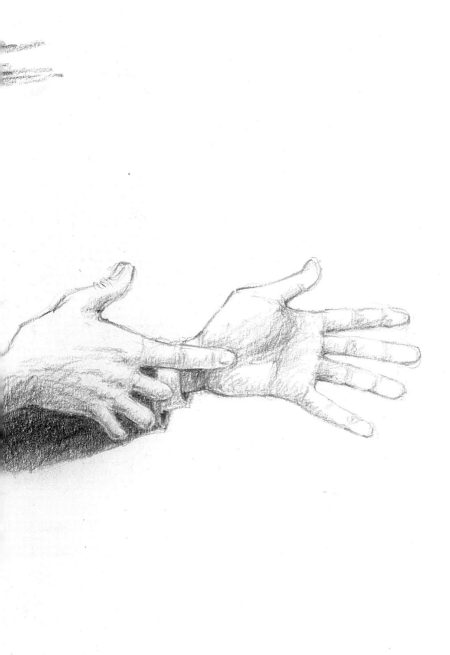

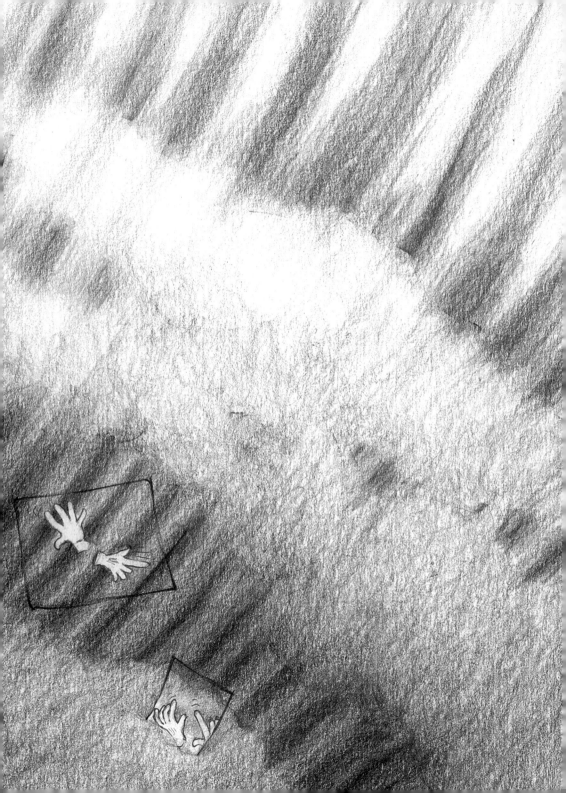

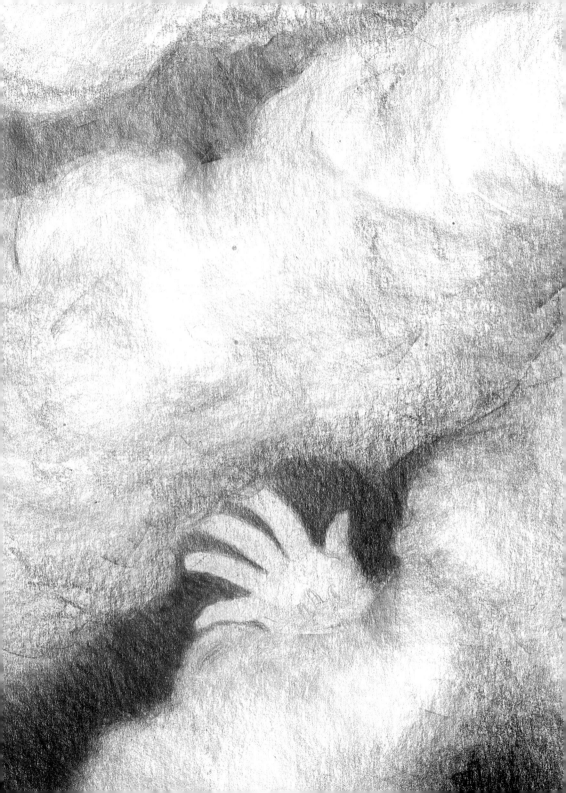

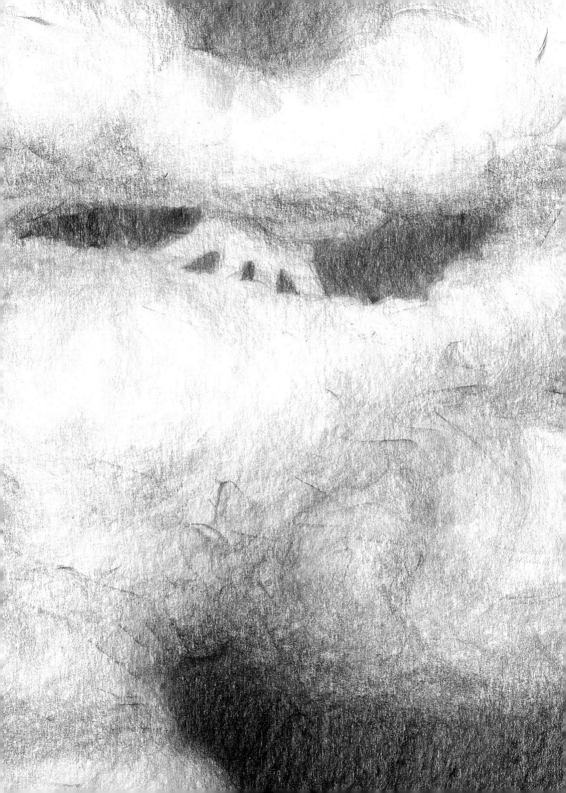

KidGlovz, what is it? What's happened?

The music, it's stopped!

What do you mean?

I can't hear music in my head. I hear nothing but silence.

Come on. We can't stay here.

LOVEGROVE'S HOUSE

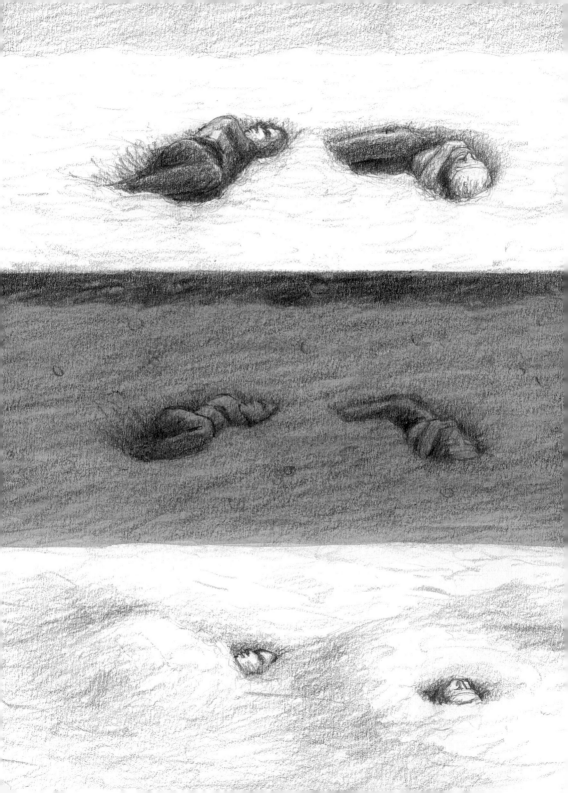

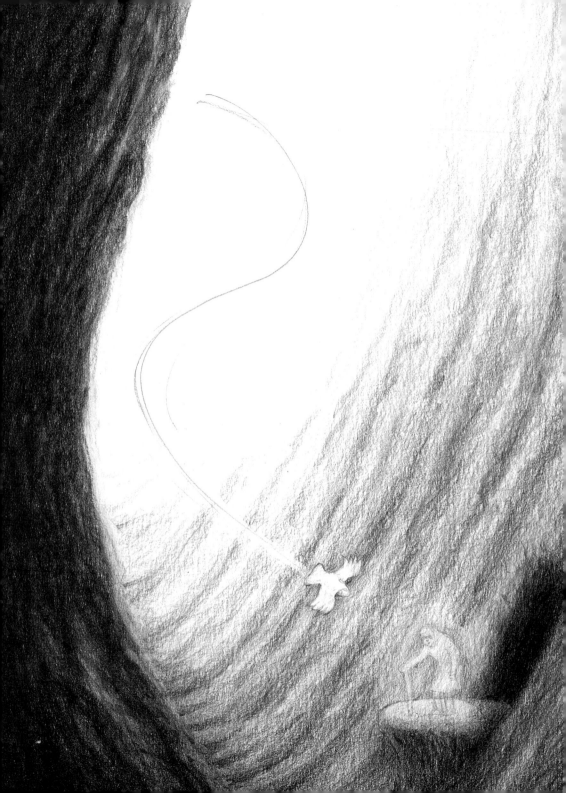

PART III

GOAT MOUNTAIN

BAA-AAA

BAA-AAA

BAA-AAA

BAA-AAA

-BAA-AAA

What's happening?

The shepherd's life is tough and bold. Our goatskin cloaks keep out the cold.

When the moon is full and the snow is deep. We sing to the goats and we sing to the sh...sh...

...sheep.

What's wrong? Don't you like our singing?

I've lost my music...

147

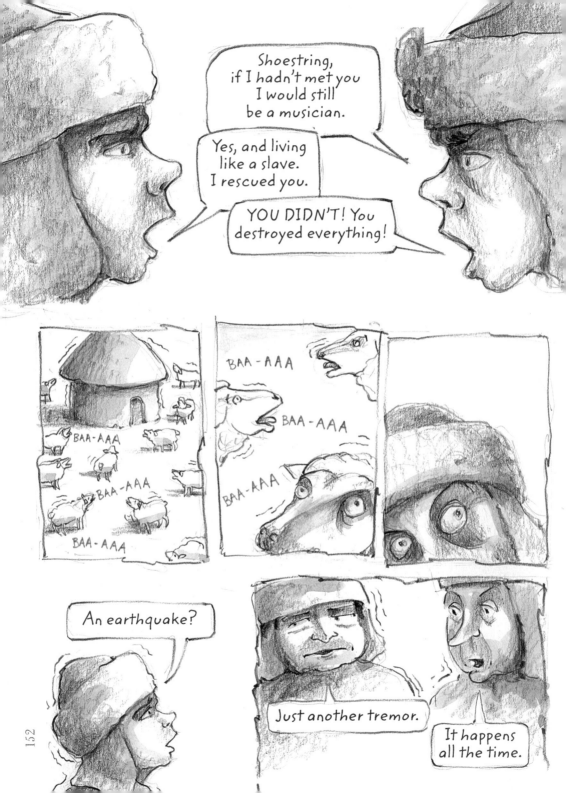

Who's Splitworld Sam?

Sometimes he's a woman. Sometimes he's a man.

You shepherds have been living in the mountains too long.

He can change his shape as fast as you can change your mind.

He can appear as a wisp of straw, a feather or a snowflake.

I don't believe in ghosts.

153

BACK IN CADENZA

INFERNO AT COUNT ARPEGGIO'S ESTATE! READ ALL ABOUT IT!

CADENZA TIMES
PRODIGY LOST IN FIRE

The Manager
Cadenza Insurance Company

Dear Sir,

With deep regret I must inform you that my dear nephew, the famous child prodigy Kidglovz, has lost his remaining fingers along with his life in a tragic fire at the estate of Count Arpeggio. He will never play piano again. According to my calculations I am entitled to compensation for the seven missing fingers, plus the loss of future income. I will also require financial recompense for the grief I have suffered in losing my dear boy in such unfortunate circumstances.

Yours most sincerely

Dr Eronious Spin

159

HUGO!

He's half frozen.

He's trembling.

Poor Hugo. He looks as if he's seen a ghost.

I have.

161

I know. We'll take him to Mot.

Mot will know what to do.

Who's Mot?

The hermit who lives on top of Goat Mountain.

They say he's 150 years old.

He can plant the sapling of knowledge in the forest of confusion.

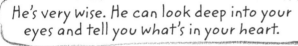

He's very wise. He can look deep into your eyes and tell you what's in your heart.

We can't go out in this weather.

We'll wait until winter ends.

MOT'S HUT

DRESSMAKER

My dreams make no sense...

Mot, are you awake?

NO. GO AWAY!

He sees the pictures in his dreams then he paints them on the walls.

No, Mot didn't paint them. They were done by the last hermit — the one before Mot.

There has always been a hermit on Goat Mountain.

179

It's the middle of the night. Can't I get any peace?

The gloves were a gift from Kid's mother!

The boy's a thief. He's stealing my dreams.

I didn't steal them. They just came to me.

They did?

Maybe you're the one.

What one?

The ONE. The next hermit. My replacement!

PART IV

I wish you wouldn't go...

I have to go.

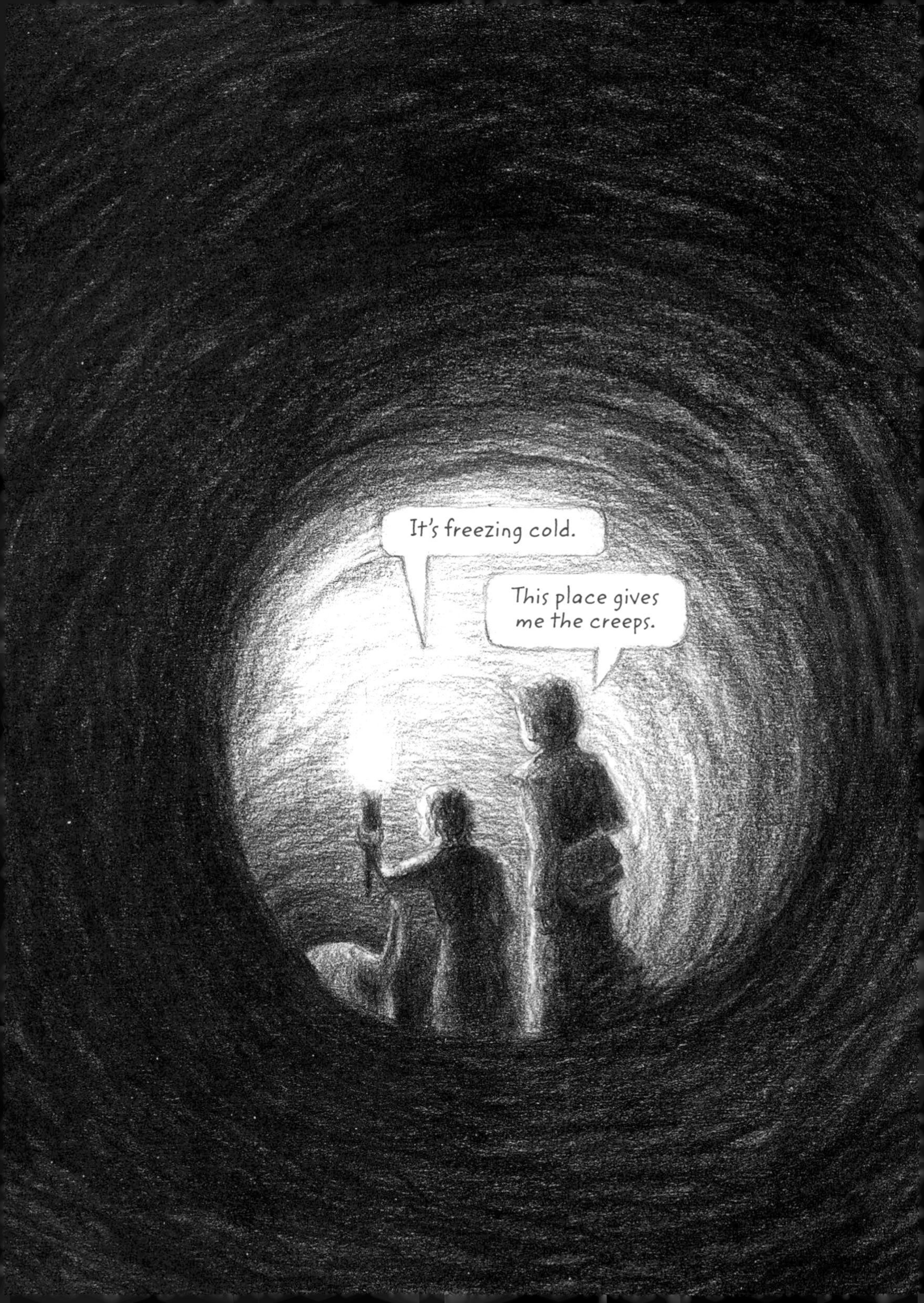
It's freezing cold.
This place gives me the creeps.

This must be the Bone Gallery.

This way.

The gloves! Grab them!

I don't like this. I want to go back.

I can't reach them. You try.

DON'T LET THEM GET AWAY!

We've lost them. Let's stop.
It must be night outside.
Let's rest here.

We've reached
the Frozen River.

It's solid ice. If only
we had wood we
could light a fire.

We have to save this for tomorrow.

Let's go back, Kid.

They don't seem to want you...

They DO want me! They're leading me somewhere.

Yes, but where?

You're just scared, Shoestring.

I want my gloves.

And you're mad. We could die here.

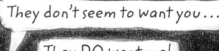

198

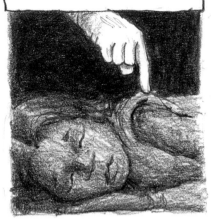

THE NEXT MORNING...

Shoestring, wake up. THEY'RE BACK!

Lost them again! Those gloves are taunting me.

Maybe they're in the power of Splitworld Sam.

I thought you didn't believe in Splitworld Sam?

I'm changing my mind. Kid, let's turn back before it's too late.

Well, we can't go on without food.

But I don't want to give up.

Let's go back. We can get more food and return.

Or you can.

All right. Lead the way, Hugo.

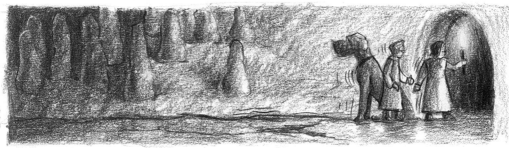

215

Where are you? I need to play in your direction.

I AM EVERYWHERE.

I'M HERE...

AND HERE...

217

Brilliant! I am myself again.

BRAVO. BRAVO. YOU HAVEN'T LOST YOUR TOUCH, KIDGLOVZ! MORE! MORE!

What will I play?

Something long to give Shoestring time to get away.

ANYTHING. DON'T STOP. LET THE CONCERT GO ON FOREVER.

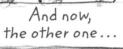
And now,
the other one...

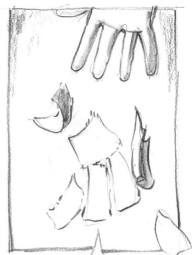

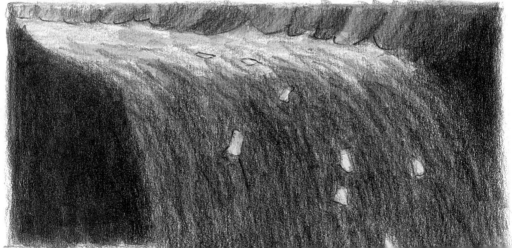

Maaa-
maa

Dado's goat!

PART V

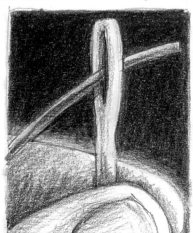

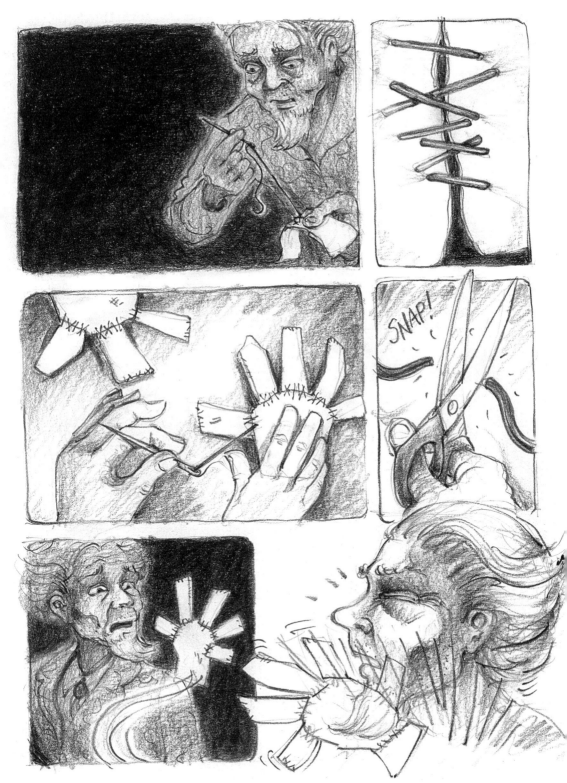

SNAP!

KidGlovz, I thought I'd never see you again!

Hugo, you found him!

Thank you, Shoestring. I knew I was right to trust you.

258

My brother told me you were dead. He collected the insurance. But you are home. Now come in — all of you.

There's something I have to do first. I'm going to see Spin. I'm not scared of him anymore. I've met worse characters than him.

Franko! What are you doing here?

New job, cousin. I'm a bodyguard.

Who are you guarding?

Dr Spin. He came into a fortune when he claimed the insurance for KidGlovz. It seems the boy was worth more to him dead than alive.

But I AM alive. I'm very much alive.

And, what's more, I've got ten fingers.

That's impossible!

I want to see my uncle.

He's not your uncle. He never was.

Boss, the kid's back!

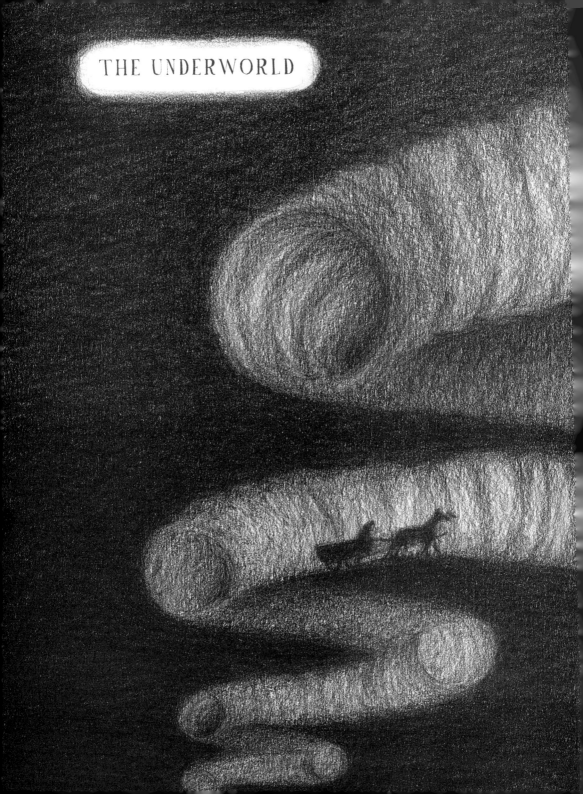

THE UNDERWORLD

There is a town
in the mountains not far
from here where people lock their
pianos on the night of the full moon.
It makes no difference – the keys move
up and down and the air is filled

with wild music...

This project has been assisted by the Australian Government
through the Australia Council, its arts funding and advisory body.

COPYRIGHTAGENCY
**CAREER
FUND**

Dale Newman would like to thank CA, the Copyright Agency, for their
support, which enabled her to attend a residency program at Pinerolo,
The Children's Book Cottage in Blackheath. Dale also wishes to thank
Margaret Hamilton for her generous support and encouragement.

First published in 2015

Allen & Unwin
83 Alexander Street Crows Nest NSW 2065 Australia
Phone: (61 2) 8425 0100
Email: info@allenandunwin.com
Web: www.allenandunwin.com

A Cataloguing-in-Publication entry is available
from the National Library of Australia
www.trove.nla.gov.au

ISBN 978 1 74237 852 7

Cover and text design by Ruth Grüner
Set in 13 pt Zemke Hand by Ruth Grüner
Colour reproduction by Splitting Image, Clayton, Victoria
This book was printed in April 2015 at Hang Tai Printing (Guang Dong) Ltd.,
Xin Cheng Ind Est, Xie Gang Town, Dong Guan, Guang Dong Province, China.

1 3 5 7 9 10 8 6 4 2

ABOUT THE AUTHOR

Julie Hunt lives on a farm in southern Tasmania
and is fascinated by landscapes and the stories they inspire.
This interest has taken her from the rugged west coast of Ireland
to the ice caves of Romania. She loves poetry, storytelling and
traditional folktales, and her own stories combine otherworldly
elements with down-to-earth humour.

Julie's novel *Song for a Scarlet Runner* was the winner of the
inaugural Readings Children's Book Prize and was shortlisted for
the CBCA Awards and the Prime Minister's Literary Award.
Her other books include a series about a plucky cowgirl called
Little Else (illustrated by Beth Norling) and the CBCA Book
of the Year, *The Coat* (illustrated by Ron Brooks) and
Precious Little (illustrated by Gaye Chapman).

www.juliehunt.com.au

ABOUT THE ILLUSTRATOR

For artist Dale Newman, the imagery in Julie's story
was so strangely familiar that drawing it into being was
a dream job for her. Dale has been engaged in creative life for
over thirty years, as a newspaper artist, a printmaker, a musician
and songwriter, a youth arts worker and a freelance illustrator.
KidGlovz is her very first-ever epic graphic novel.

Dale lives on the NSW south coast with her partner and son,
who kindly agreed to model for the book. Her artwork also
appears on the cover of Julie's award-winning novel
Song for a Scarlet Runner.

www.dalenewman.com.au

Many thanks to Erica Wagner, Sue Flockhart
and Ruth Grüner, whose superb talents helped create
the music in this book. Thanks from Dale to Alison
Rutherford, Ann James, and to Julie Hunt,
for the gift of her story.